INDIAN CASTE SYSTEM

A STUDY

BY

C. HAYAVADANA RAO

WITH A FOREWORD BY

R. WADIA

Low Price Publications
2014

Conjeevaram Hayavadana Rao (1865-1946)

First Published 1931
Reprinted in **LPP** 2014

ISBN 10: 81-7536-540-4
ISBN 13: 978-81-7536-540-7

Published by
Low Price Publications
A-6, 2nd Floor, Nimri Commercial Centre,
Ashok Vihar Phase 4, Delhi 110052 (INDIA)
tel.: +91.11.27302453 fax.: +91.11.47061936
url: www.LPPindia.com e-mail: info@LPPindia.com

Printed at
IIP Printers
Delhi

PRINTED IN INDIA

PREFACE

In issuing this little book on a subject of great complexity but of considerable practical value, I have been guided mainly by two considerations: first, that what has been said on it by observers and writers of some authority should be more widely known among those who are desirous of seriously studying it; and secondly, that the lines that research into it should take hereafter should, if possible, be clearly grasped before any tangible results could be hoped for from it. While no originality whatever is claimed for what is contained in the volume, readers will perceive that no pains have been spared to state the theories concerned in as clear a manner as possible and to limit their discussion to the barest dimensions possible. This, it is hoped, will prove an advantage to those interested in the subject. They would for one thing, be enabled to see the wood from the trees, and thus be helped to probe further into the subject. The topic too is so vast and so important, from a social, and, let me add, scientific point of view, that greater attention deserves to be given to it than it has so far received from scholars in this country.

I am deeply indebted to Professor Wadia not only for the personal interest he evinced in the subject-matter of this book, when it first appeared in a series of articles in the *Mysore Economic Journal*, but also for the readiness with which he undertook to introduce it to the larger public engaged in the study of socio-economic matters.

In the preparation of the Index and the passing of the proofs to the Press, I have derived valuable help from Mr. B. Garudachar, Chief Examiner, Bangalore Press, which I desire to acknowledge here.

BANGALORE, *8th Nov. 1931.* C. HAYAVADANA RAO.

FOREWORD

There is nothing so unique in India, nothing so all-pervasive in India as *caste*. Normally one may expect that so common a theme would be as well understood as it is talked about. But it does not take one long to discover how involved it is and how ignorant we are about it. Some good research has been done throwing some light on its complexity, but a goodly portion of it lies buried in census reports or learned tomes, and the man in the street, even an educated one, knows precious little about it. That is why I felt very much interested in the articles on caste, which appeared in the pages of the *Mysore Economic Journal* from the well-known pen of Mr. C. Hayavadana Rao. It is a very happy idea to republish them in book form, and I for one particularly welcome it. With the modesty of a scholar, Mr. Hayavadana Rao has resisted the temptation to take sides, to condemn it as satanic or laud it as divine. He has not aspired to give a new theory or bless any old theory relating to caste. He has been content to give a very lucid summary of the theories developed by different scholars, both Indian and European. The busiest man can spare some time to go through a booklet of 77 pages, and with such an aid to knowledge, no educated Indian would be justified in saying that he knows nothing about caste. Too often has it been taken for granted that caste has always been a fixed entity, above all change. As a matter of fact, like everything else on the face of the earth, caste underwent changes, as varied and as deep as they could possibly have been. Once the educated Hindu grasps this fact, he will have a better perspective to judge its worth and to consider critically what is living and what is dead in it. Mr. Hayavadana Rao has suggested various lines on which further research is still anxiously awaited. I trust his appeal will not fall on deaf ears. If his little book stimulates an intelligent interest in the subject, I am sure none will be more pleased with it than the author himself, and he will have earned our most grateful thanks.

THE UNIVERSITY,
MYSORE,
23rd October 1931.

A. R. WADIA.

CONTENTS

Indian Caste System : A Study.

CHAPTER I.

Historical Study of Caste.

Introductory—Relation of Caste to Race—Sir Edward Gait's Opinion—Caste System in South India.

INTRODUCTORY.

THE subject of Indian Caste is a highly interesting one, but it bristles with difficulties. But its very complexities should, I think, induce economists and sociologists to study it with care and attention. In this little book, I propose only to lead the way towards a better elucidation of the subject. An attempt—and no more than an attempt is possible—will be made in it to probe some of the problems connected with it. The relationship of caste to race; the theories as to its origin, the original Indian theories and the recent European theories; and some of the effects of the caste as a socio-religious system will be among the points that will be touched upon it. No finality is claimed for any of the views propounded or conclusions arrived at in it. Whatever is stated is only put forward in the form of a tentative hypothesis and if the facts adduced do not support any of the views advanced, they may be discarded. One thing, however, I would suggest in this connection. It is this: A historical study of caste is still a desideratum. A study of the materials available in the Vedas, the Buddhist Texts, the later Sanskrit literature is, of course, necessary. Weber, Oldenberg, Rhys Davids have contributed much towards this study. But for the development of caste during post-Buddhistic age down to the eighteenth century, we have still an amount of matter locked up in the rich vernacular literatures of India that deserves to be carefully sifted. There is here a fertile field of work for research students in our country. Until this work is undertaken, I do not think anything final can be said on this much debated subject of caste. The field is vast and the workers are few. Hence my appeal for more work in this department of research.

Relation of Caste to Race.

The relation of caste to race has been much discussed but this is hardly the occasion to go in any detail into the many conflicting theories which have been propounded in regard to it. At one extreme is the theory of Nesfield who assumes the essential unity of the Indian race denies in general any difference of blood between Aryan and Aboriginal and holds that caste is merely a question of occupation. According to him, by the time the caste system and its restriction on marriage had been evolved, the Aryan blood had already been absorbed beyond recovery into the indigenous, so that no caste, not even the Brahman, could claim to have sprung from Aryan ancestors. The existing differences in social rank are due solely to the character of the occupation; the scavenger castes are at the bottom of the social scale, then those engaged in hunting and fishing, and so on, through a regular gradation, to the landowners and warriors, and at the top of all, the priests. The antithesis of this theory is Sir Herbert Risley's view that the primary distinction was one of race, engendered by the contact of the conquering fair-skinned Aryans and the conquered black aborigines. The former despise the latter, but at first, having too few women of their own they were often obliged to take aboriginal girls as their wives. Later on, when this scarcity no longer existed, they closed their ranks to any further intermixture; and when they did this, each group became a caste like those of the present day. There was a regular gradation of social rank, the communities of pure Aryan and aboriginal stock being respectively at the top and bottom, and those with varying degrees of racial mixture in the middle. Once started the principle of endogamy was strengthened and extended to groups formed otherwise than on a racial basis until the modern multiplicity of caste was evolved. But even now caste largely corresponds to race; and the social status of the caste is indicated by its physical type, those of the top having an Aryan and those at the bottom an aboriginal physiognomy. Taking the nose as the most characteristic feature, Sir Herbert propounded that castes vary in social rank according to the average nasal index of their members. It did not, of course, mean each individual caste had its distinctive physical type but that each social stratum comprising a number of castes of similar standing can be distinguished in this way from those above and below it. It seems necessary to add as Sir Edward Gait well points out, that Risley used the expression 'Aryan' to designate the people calling themselves *Arya* or *Noble* who entered India from beyond the North-West Frontier and brought with them the Sanskritic languages and the religious ideas to which expression is given in the Vedas and Upanishads, and whose physical type is represented by that of the Jats and Rajputs, *viz.*, a long head, a straight finely cut nose, a long, symmetrically narrow face, a well-developed forehead, regular features and high facial angle. He refused to enter on the controversy between those who, like Posche and Penka, regard the tall, blonde, dolichocephalic and leptorrhine Scandinavian as representing the primitive Aryan type and those like Isaac Taylor, have held that it is to be identified with the short-headed leptorrhine neolithic race who built the dwellings of South Germany, Switzerland and Northern Italy

Risley's conclusions have, however, not gained general acceptance. Based on the measurements made by him in Bengal, they have been called in question by Crooke in the United Provinces, Enthoven in Bombay, and Thurston in Madras, while O'Donnell has argued that even the Bengal measurements are often at variance with it. On the other hand, Nesfield's theory of racial unity is conclusively disproved by the measurements which show considerable diversity, not only in different areas but also amongst different groups of castes in the same area. It is not proposed to go into this large question here except to point out that Sir Herbert Risley has, according to competent critics, exaggerated the isolation of the present grouping of the people and that caste, in its modern rigid form, is of comparatively recent origin. The older custom, for instance, recognizes the possibility of a Kshatriya becoming a Brahman or *vice versa* and although a man is supposed to take his first wife from his own class, there was no binding rule to this effect, while in any case he was free to take a second wife from a lower class. As Mr. Crooke points out similar laxities of practice prevail at the present time among certain communities in the Himalayan Districts of the Punjab. Caste, again, has been habitually modified by the action of Rajahs who have not infrequently claimed the right of promoting and degrading members of the various castes. The process of amalgamation of castes and tribal groups is specially observable in the case of forest tribes when they come in contact with Hinduism. Each of them shows, as Mr. Crooke puts it, a ragged fringe in which the more primitive tribe is found intermingled with the more civilized race.

Sir Edward Gait's Opinion.

Writing of the extreme mutability of caste, Sir Edward Gait says :—" Those which I have described as discontinuous whereby a whole community raises its social rank, though disturbing the correlation between caste and status which Risley alleged to exist, have in themselves no effect on the racial composition of the community unless in time the upstarts succeed in intermarrying with some other social group. But the changes arising from the transfer of individuals or groups from one caste to another would clearly disturb the homogeneity of the castes receiving them. This would be the case, for instance, where the men are in the habit of taking wives from other castes of lower status. Still more would it be the case amongst the functional castes. If it be conceded that such castes have received successive accretions of groups from outside, it follows that the main caste is seldom a homogeneous body and that measurements taken, as they have almost invariably been, without regard to the sub-caste, cannot be expected to give uniform results. The individual sub-castes are more likely to consist of persons having a common origin but this is also by no means an invariable rule. The processes of fission have no doubt been in operation from the earliest times ; and the sub-castes of to-day, though more uniform in type than the castes of which they form part, were probably in their turn formed out of different groups, which, in course of time, have become so closely intermingled that all traces of the original distinctions have disappeared."

If many of the existing castes have a functional origin, can there be any possible correspondence between caste and race? "The answer is," says Sir Edward Gait, "that the conquerors would have reserved for themselves the higher occupations, leaving the more primitive warriors and traders; on the other, hunters, fishermen, basket-makers, scavengers and agrestic serfs. Handicrafts and other intermediate occupations would be followed by the half-breeds who were in closer contact with the conquerors than the pure aborigines. Again, not only would persons of higher status monopolize the occupations regarded by them as superior, but the occupations themselves would be graded in public estimation according to the status of the person practising them. This, of course, is merely an indication of the general tendency. As is known, there can be no doubt that aboriginal priests have often obtained recognition as Brahmans and aboriginal chieftains as Kshatriyas, just as some outcastes from the conquering race no doubt found an asylum amongst the aborigines. When members of one caste take to the occupation of another, it would ordinarily be the case that both communities occupy more or less the same social position. It would be much easier for an artisan to take a handicraft other than his own than for a scavenger or boatman to adopt it as his means of livelihood. Such accretions, therefore, would not necessarily affect materially the racial composition of the caste receiving them."

Caste System in South India.

In writing as above Sir Edward Gait takes care to explain that his remarks "apply primarily to Northern India". "In the South," he adds, "the infusion of Aryan and other foreign bloods is much weaker and there is far greater racial uniformity." While this statement is not borne out by the figures furnished by Mr. Thurston, there is no doubt that caste has been more rigid in Southern India. The peculiar physical division of the country may have helped much in the maintenance of caste. During pre-British days it is possible that Hindu kings and chiefs exercised considerable power in connection with the regulation of caste rules and rights. Whether they included the power of promotion from a lower to a higher caste, as Hindu chiefs in Northern India, especially in the Punjab, still do, is a matter for further investigation. If the powers now vielded by the Hindu rulers in the West Coast is any guide in the matter, it may be inferred that such promotion and degradation was common in Southern India, in olden days as it was, and is to some extent in Northern India. It is on some such basis as this that

Mr. Thurston's figures are capable of a rational explanation. They plainly indicate wide-spread miscegenation through a wide extent of a country during a prolonged period. This view is supported to some extent by the *dictum* of the Hindu Law-givers from the earliest times. Thus Baudhayana in his *Dharma-sutras* (I. 1. 32-33) includes the inhabitants of Dakshinapada (the south) among those of "mixed origin". Hemadri, who wrote in the thirteenth century A.D., in his *Sraddhakalpa*, quotes the following text from the *Saura Purana* :—"The Brahmans of Anga, Vanga, Kalinga, Saurashtra, Gurjara, Abhira, Konkani, Dravida, Dakshinapatha, Avanti and Magadha should be avoided." Can the pre-platyrrhine nose of the several of the Brahman sects be traced to their mixed origin ?

CHAPTER II.

Origin of Caste: Brahmanism.

Brahmanism—Sir Denzil Ibbetson's Views—Sir Alfred Lyall's Views.

It is possible to imagine a period of time in the history of South India where there were no Brahmans in it. The Brahmans were introduced into it, according to tradition, about the third century A.D. But it is probable that there were already some in the country at the time of, or prior to, the Buddhist king Asoka whose inscriptions (third century B.C.) have been found in the State. At any rate it is inferable from lithic inscriptions found in the Mysore State that the Brahmans were in the country by about the first century A.D. Before their advent what was the nature of the social order that prevailed? In what terms should we describe it? This is an interesting question, but it is hardly possible to pursue it here. It is possible that the people were already divided into tribes as among all primitive societies. They had probably also developed guilds based upon hereditary occupation. It is not impossible, too, that they had by themselves evolved to some extent the priestly office as well. The effect of the higher type of religion brought into their midst by the Brahmans had probably the effect of exalting the priestly office to an extent unknown before in the land and of strengthening belief in the hereditary nature of the occupation. In course of time as social intercourse increased in diverse ways, this principle should have received support by the elaboration from the theories of Brahmanical text-writers and legists—like Manu, Baudhayana and the rest—of a set of rules, regulating marriage, intermarriage, declaring certain kinds of foods and occupations to be impure and polluting and prescribing conditions and degree of social intercourse between the several classes of people.

SIR DENZIL IBBETSON'S VIEWS.

"Add to these the pride of social rank and the pride of blood which," as Sir Denzil Ibbetson observes, "are natural to man and which alone would reconcile a nation to restriction, at once irksome from a domestic and burdensome from a material point of view, and it is hardly to be wondered at that caste should have assumed the rigidity which distinguishes it in India." It undoubtedly should have taken ages for this rigidity to become an accomplished fact. First Jainism and then Buddhism, both of which are known to have flourished in the State from about the fourth century B.C. at least must have impeded caste development itself to some extent. But the decline of these faiths and the practical reassertion of the Vedic faith by the renowned Sankaracharya (eighth century A.D.), who made

Sringeri in Mysore his chief pontifical seat, must have been followed by a silent reversion to, if not a re-establishment of the old social order. The Virasaiva revival under Basava in the middle of the twelfth century A.D. was no doubt a protest against the growing caste spirit in the land. That this movement which started not far away at Kalyan, in the Kannada country, found many adherents in the State including the Rajas of Mysore and Coorg and numerous minor chiefs, shows the appeal that it made to the popular mind. The revival of Vedic faith which had ere this begun in the State with the advent of the Vaishnavite reformer Ramanujacharya (twelfth century A.D.), who had sought refuge in the Mysore country from the persecution of the neighbouring Chola king and had converted the local Jain king to his faith and founded his seat at Melkote, near French Rocks, was signalized by the partial wiping out of caste inequalities. Apart from his philosophical teachings, Ramanujacharya in keeping with the times, preached a social equality which imparted a new vitality to the old Vedic faith. In this he no doubt built upon the older foundations of his precursors, Alvars, who had scoured the country and preached the religion of love to all in the land. Vaishnavism checked by its very concession of practical, if only partial, equality of all persons, made caste lose not a little of its old vigour. A similar effect was produced by the teachings of Madhvacharya (thirteenth century) who taught equality was to be cherished not merely in the social sphere but also in the religious. He held that Siva and Vishnu were equally adorable and that devotion to God enabled everyone to attain salvation. He forbade altogether animal sacrifices, thus absorbing into the old Vedic religion the most practical part of the decaying Jain and Buddhist faiths. There is reason to believe that for at least the next two centuries and a half (1336-1565) during which the Hindu kings of Vijayanagar bore supreme sway over the whole of Southern India, including the Mysore State which was ruled over by one of their Viceroys, caste must have been an intolerably bearable sort of institution. Inscriptions show that these kings were as supreme in religious and social matters as in political. As the Cholas had done before them, they relaxed the restrictions of caste in the case of the people who rose in social scale. They even remitted in their cases certain taxes which, as members of the castes to which they belonged, they had to bear. The break-up of the Vijayanagar kingdom by the conquest of the south byMuhammadan rulers from the north tightened and strengthened rather than relaxed the bonds of caste. This conquest deprived the people of the support of their own time-honoured rulers in the settlement of their social and religious questions. Brahman expounders of law and usage lost the services of the curt authority to which they have long been accustomed to look for sanctioning a necessary change in religious or social matters. These changes were issued not infrequently in the guise of civil or political edicts or charters granted to the leaders of particular castes. What the religious movements of the many centuries preceding the Muhammadan advent had done in softening, if not entirely breaking, the fetters of caste, was, as it were, lost. The hardening of social bonds has been continued in a more pronounced form since the consolidation of British rule in India, a rule which has made religious neutrality a basic principle of its political policy. Society soon reached a stage of arrested development in which no voices were heard except those from the tomb. Natural re-adjustment of social difficulties had become all but impossible in the new condition of society. People thus left to their own resources, had perforce to improvise remedies to meet difficulties that arose from time to time. In the absence of civil authorities interested in social and religious matters, they naturally looked to the Brahman as the leader of society, for a way out. In cases in which he was found unaccommodating—and there were many—they organized themselves on new lines and challenged the supremacy of the Brahman himself. Even those who professed to belong to religions which originated in a protest against caste as such took a line diametrically opposed to their tenets. The further desire of many castes to come under the one or the other of the four traditional castes of Manu has also been strongly marked. These and other tendencies which ended in hardening caste and making it more burdensome have been frequently referred to by Census Superintendents of Mysore and Madras.

SIR ALFRED LYALL'S VIEWS.

The tendencies above referred to testify to the vitality of Brahmanism—understanding by that term the system of social and religious belief which places the Brahman at the head—in Mysore as anywhere else in India. They cannot but recall the oft-quoted words of Sir Alfred Lyall in which he describes how Brahmanism has been silently absorbing the many millions of India. He traces the proselytising tendency of Brahmanism to three causes all of which have had—and are still having even now—their effect in Mysore. These are: (1) That it is indigenous, the produce of the soil and of the environment that still exists. (2) That it is a social system and a very elastic one; while the people of India as a body still need a religion which, like Brahmanism, provides them with social rules, with laws of custom as well as of conduct. (3) That it encourages and is nourished by a constant miraculous agency working at full pressure and by relays of divine embodiments, while in the present intellectual state of the population in India no religion will be widely embraced without visible miraculous credentials. Sir Alfred adds that "it may fairly be conjectured that these characters are likely to keep Brahmanism alive in India for several generations to come. No one need doubt that it is gradually becoming purged and refined but this is a process through which all popular religions pass; and they are not always extinguished by it." The actual process of absorption into Brahmanism, "the Brahmanizing of the original non-Aryan or casteless tribes" is thus described by him:—

"The clans and races, which inhabit the hill tracts, the outlying uplands and the uncleared jungle districts of India, are melting into Hinduism all over India by a process much more rapid and effective than individual conversions. Among all those aboriginal or non-Aryan communities a continued social change is going on; they alter their modes of life to suit improved conditions of existence; their languages decay, and they gradually go over to the dominant Aryan rituals. They pass into Brahmanists by a natural upward transition which leads them to adopt the religion of the castes immediately above them in the social scale of the composite population among which they settle down. And we may reasonably guess that this process has been working for centuries, though it is likely to have been much more rapid than ever under British Rule. The 'Ethnical Frontier' described in the Annals of Rural Bengal is an ever-breaking shore of primitive beliefs which compel constantly into the ocean of Brahmanism; and when Mr. W.W. Hunter in his dissertation on the Non-Aryan languages in India describes the gradations by which the acknowledged non-Aryans of the highlands slide into low caste Hindus of the plain, he describes a transmutation that is going on all over India. In Central India it has certainly gone very far, with a speed that seems to increase. In the interior of the Eastern Himalayas the Buddhists dispute with the Brahmans over the mountain clans and the sparse families that live in the habitable glens; but on the southern slopes, and in the jungles that spring the bases of the hills, the

Brahmans are prevailing unopposed. For all these tribes, by becoming Hindu, come under the Brahmans ; and whenever they have succeeded so far as to found a State as the Gurkhas founded Nepal, they have established the predominancy of caste and creed as a State religion. The number of converts thus added to Brahmanism in the last few generations especially in this country must be immense : and if the word proselyte may be used in the sense of one who has come, and who has been readily admitted, not necessarily being one that has been invited or persuaded to come, then Brahmanism might lay claim to by far the most successful proselytising religion of modern times in India.

Thus Brahmanism is all over India a necessary first stage for the outlying tribes towards Indian civilization, or admission to the citizenship of the great Hindu community ; it very rarely implies any ethical chance, or even a formal abandonment of one ritual for another ; it is usually a rapid sliding into Hindu customs and an attempt at social assimilation. But the complete process thus necessitates a considerable change of worship and race of life ; for perhaps the surest sign of a family reception into Brahmanism, that whereas the Brahman formerly was never called in, he is latterly found officiating at domestic epochs and ceremonies, of birth, marriage, or death. This implies conformity to Brahmanic rules of eating, intermarriages and the like, and the evolution of a caste or sub-caste. If the converted family are standing among their own people, the Brahman for a consideration proportionate to the emergency of complexity of the case, will usually discover for them a descent Hindu pedigree, or (what is much easier) a miraculous incident which proves a half savage chief or rich outcastes to be really allied to one of recognized castes. We know how readily the Gods are always intervened to explain away awkward incidents of birth and provide a great man of humble origin with a parentage better suited to the success. Thus the Gond chiefs of the Central India highlands all now claim Rajput ancestry, and have ranked themselves in the soldier caste. In aspiration they are now Hindus of the Hindus, some of them carrying ceremonial refinement to the highest pitch of purism; but nevertheless they are really no better than recent parvenus from the clans which still run almost wild in adjacent hills and forests, and which are nothing for Bráhmans or caste prejudices. It is calculated that the Bheels, a tribe widely spread over Central India, must have been passing over in large numbers to Brahmanism during the present century. There is a tribe near Ajmere, of whom half were forcibly made Mussalmans, while the other half held its own non-Hindu customs, and until very lately intermarried with its Mussalman kindred; but now this last mentioned half has Brahmanized, and would no more marry with Mussalmans than the Raja of Benares. Sir George Campbell, in his Report upon the Government of Bengal, in 1871-72, wrote: "It is a great mistake to suppose that the Hindu religion is not proselytising; the system of caste gives room for the introduction of any of its outsiders. So long as people do not interfere with existing castes, they may form a new caste and call themselves Hindus; and the Brahmans are always ready to receive all who will submit to them and pay them. The process of manufacturing Rajputs from ambitious aborigines goes on before our eyes." This passage which the Lecturer has quoted, is one recently recorded observation out of many that might be produced, of the operation of that process which I have called the first mode of Brahmanic propagation. Almost the whole of the great province of Assam, in the north-east of Bengal, conquered and settled by people from across the eastern frontiers of India, supposed to be akin to the Siamese, is said to have become Brahmanized during the last two centuries. It may be granted that people who come in after this fashion do not fulfil the meaning with which the term proselyte is used in describing the operations of a professedly missionary faith, and that Professor Max Muller in his lecture clearly used the term in this, the ordinary European, meaning. Nevertheless, when we undertake to estimate the vitality of a religion, and its capacity for future adaptation and development (without which no religion can endure long), we must consider and take account of growth by agglomeration, as well as of extension by missionary zeal. And it is fair to argue that a religion which still possesses so much power of extension and assimilation as Brahmanism, which has constantly produced, and is continually producing, reformers and revivalists, cannot safely be set out of all calculation in forecasting the religious future of Asia, a problem so prodigiously complex and obscure."

The process of absorption so graphically described above has been in full operation in the South of India including Mysore—as evidenced by the passages I have quoted from the Census Reports of Madras and Mysore. It is an undoubted fact that Brahmanism is expansive though it is proselytising rather than missionary, and it proselytises " by absorbing tribes, not by converting individuals "

CHAPTER III.

Origin of Caste: Some Early Theories.

Origin of Caste—Sir Alfred Lyall's Theory—Sir Herbert Risley's Theory—Sir Henry Sumner Maine's Theory—Sir Denzil Ibbetson's Theory—Critics of his Theory.

The origin of caste, whose development has been briefly touched upon already, has given rise to much speculation. The many theories which have been put forward in regard to it have sometimes mistaken development for origins proper. Modern theorists have differed so much from each other and have elaborated their views at such length that it is not possible to attempt more here than a brief reference to them. The historian, Mill, has suggested that the original division must have been the work of some inspired individual, a legislator, or a social reformer who perceived the advantages that would result from a systematic division of labour. The subordination of castes he accounts for by the superstitious terror and the designing lust of power which have so frequently been invoked to explain the natural supremacy of the religious class. Because the ravages of war were dreaded most after the calamities sent by heaven, he finds that the military class properly occupy the second place. This arrangement he apparently contemplates as at no time either necessary or wholesome and as finally destroyed by the degradations which the multiplications of trades made inevitable. Heeren and Klaproth have contended that the division into castes is founded on an original diversity of race, and that the higher castes are possessed of superior beauty. The clear complexion and regular features of the Brahmans are said to distinguish them as completely from the Sudras as the Spanish Creoles were distinguished from the Peruvians. This explanation is, however, generally conjoined with that founded on the tradition of conquest by the higher castes. It is suggested in this connection that the three castes of higher colour (*Trivarnika*)—the white Brahmans, the red Kshatriyas, the yellow Vaisyas—are at least in the early hymns and the *Brahmanas* spoken as the Aryas, the Sanskrit-speaking conquerors, in contradistinction to the dark of the aborigines, the Dasyus. In fact, Arya, which means householder, was, it is added, the original name of the largest caste now called the Vaisyas. Roth holds that the Vedic people advanced from their home in the Punjab, drove the aborigines into the hills, and took possession of the country lying between the Ganges, the Jumna and the Vindhya Range. "In this stage of complication and disturbance," says he, "power naturally fell into the hands of those who did not possess any direct authority," *i. e.*, the domestic priests of the numerous tribal kings. "The Sudras," he regards "as a conquered race, perhaps a branch of the Aryan stock, which immigrated at an earlier period into India, perhaps an autochthonous Indian tribe." The hypothesis is slightly modified by Meiners, who supposes that instead of one conquest there may have been two successive immigrations—the first immigrants being subdued by the second, and then forming an intermediate class between their conquerors and their aborigines; or if there were no aborigines, the mixture of the two immigrant races would form an intermediate class. In the same way Mr. Talboys Wheeler suggests that the Sudras may be the original conquerors of the race now represented by the Pariahs. Criticising these theories, Mr. W. E. Smith, the author of the article on *Caste* in the last edition of the *Encyclopædia Brittanica*, says that most of these suggestions and explanations seem rather to describe the mode in which the existing institutions of caste might be transplanted from one land to another, from a mother-land to its colonies, and altered by its new conditions. Military conquest though it often introduces servitude does not naturally lead to the elevation of the priesthood. "It is unscientific to assume large historical events, or large ethnological facts, or the existence of some creator of Social Order." Mr. Smith also combats the view of Roth that the Sudras might be an autochthonous Indian tribe. He says that this hypothesis is opposed to the fact that, while the Sudra is debarred from sharing important Vedic sacrifices, the Bhagavata Purana expressly permits him to sacrifice "without mantras" and imposes on him duties with reference to Brahmans and cows which one would not expect in the case of a nation strange in blood. While the subordination of the Kshatriya, who *ex hypothesi* should have contributed most to the conquest, the Brahman, is not quite intelligible to him, except on the basis of a previous subordination of castes among the conquerors, he thinks that the position of the Sudra certainly suggests conquest. "But are there," he asks, "sound historical reasons for supposing that Brahmans and Sudras belonged to different nations, or that either class was confined to one nation?" Professors Macdonnell and Keith agree in thinking that "it is reasonable to reckon the Sudra of the later texts as belonging to the aborigines who had been reduced to subjection by the Aryans." Mr. Rama Prasad Chanda, an Indian scholar, writing recently, disputes this view and suggests that the status of a Sudra of the later Vedic age was like that of slaves or serfs of Europe. He thinks that the internecine wars of the Aryans themselves ended in the taking of war-captives who eventually became slaves. It is known that these wars lasted into the period of the later *Samhitas* and *Brahmanas*. War-captives, whether of the Aryan or Dasyu race, were, according to him, treated alike and turned into slaves. He quotes Manu (VIII—415) to show that this mode of making slaves was a well-recognized one. Zimmer may be said to take a similar view. Difference of caste, according to him, has arisen partly out of religious distinctions, partly out of racial and tribal differences and still more out of hereditary crafts, occupations and modes of life. In the Vedas we only see the beginnings of such a system. But long before any ideas of religious and ceremonial distinction was developed, the tribes appear to have recognized a certain 'classification' which in fact became the foundation of the caste system. There were, from the first, priests, or rather, singers of those sacred hymns and invocations, the proper use of which had the great effect in securing victory and abundant spoil. And the course of adventure which the advancing tribes were pursuing would not fail to bring into prominence the warrior class—especially those noble and distinguished families which gave birth to the natural leaders of the clans, and which afterwards furnished the Rajahs and Chiefs who arose out of the earlier tribal organization. These two classes grew into the 'twice-born' (Brahman and Kshatriya) castes. These two chief castes apart, all the bulk of the people are merely spoken of as *Vis*, which later became *Vaisya*, *i.e.*, 'the (Aryan) common people'. Every invading army or colonizing nation, however, comes with a host of camp followers and inferiors probably of various origin; among the Aryans some had apparently been admitted at least to the outer courts of the community, and had conformed to Aryan customs. Accordingly as the settlement progressed, so another (fourth) group came to be distinguished. Perhaps one of the tribes early admitted within the Aryan pale may have originally had the name Sudra; or it is possible that some of the camp followers or serfs were called by that name. As the Aryans settled down, mixed races began to grow up. The Aryan influence indeed extended as much by mixed marriages, alliances and conversions, as by direct conquest. Before long the converted aboriginal and mixed races acknowledging Hindu customs alike required a new name; they became fused with one general class, and were called *Sudras*. The races who were not received into the pale at all remained 'outcastes'. These broad divisions soon came to be split up into many groups, and into subdivisions innumerable and the old general names remained chiefly in the books, and were used as generic terms rather than as actual caste-names.

Sir Alfred Lyall's Theory.

Arguing from a different point of view, Sir Alfred Lyall comes to the conclusion that caste is posterior to the tribe. "It would seem to be a reasonable theory," he suggests, "that the caste as an institution, is of a later formation than the tribe. For, so far as the actual course of things can be watched, in early and wild times a tribe or clan regularly throws off another tribe or clan after its own kind as swarms come out of a wild bee's nest, the state of the world being favourable to the existence of such groups. But there comes a later period when the pressure of powerful dynasties and the rise of industrial bodies render tribal formations no longer possible, driving men into peaceful pursuits and swallowing up petty independencies. In the Western world, these agencies rapidly obliterated the tribes, and gradually produced the modern population pounded up and measured out into nationalities with their kinship narrowed down to the immediate family and the prohibited degrees very closely down. In India religion seems to have stepped in as the tribal institutions dissolved, and to have stung all the kindred groups upon the great circle which call caste. Within a caste the inner rings of consanguinity survive but in a stunted condition as compared with a clan within a tribe, it being obviously impossible that in this altered phase of society the kindred groups should continue to hold together by the fiction of descent from a common stock. The folk take to various occupations, inhabit different places, contract strange marriages, worship other Gods ; the ups and downs of more complicated life break short the pedigree, sever the kinship and rub off the patronymic ; the distant branches of a family fall out of sight and the long genealogies of the clan give place to the comparatively narrow tables of prohibited degrees which prevail among castes. Then the trade, or the profession or the common ritual becomes the bond union instead of descent or political association, and thus the mixed population of India may have re-arranged itself into castes, propelled into those grooves by the archaic and inveterate exclusiveness of primitive Asiatics regarding marriage and food. You must not marry one of your own blood but neither must you marry a stranger of unknown descent and foreign habits; your caste means those with whom you may safely inter-marry and share food without risk of incurring some unlucky taint which may give you much trouble in the existence and the next."

SIR HERBERT RISLEY'S THEORY.

This theory of caste originating from the tribe has, however, not gained general acceptance. Sir Herbert Risley says that "the conjecture seems at first sight plausible; but a glance at the facts will show that the transformation in question is confined to those tribes which have been brought into contact with the regular caste system, and have adopted its characteristic usages from religious or social motives. The Manipuris, for example, were converted from Nagas into Hindus only a century or two ago; and I am informed that the family archives of the Raja contain an account of the process by which the change was effected. The Bhumii, again, were a tribe at a still more recent date, and retain plentiful traces of their origin. On the other hand, the races of Baluchistan, where Hindu influence is practically non-existent, show no inclination to follow the example of the Indian Muhammadans and organize themselves on the model of caste. The primitive tribe in fact, wherever we find it, is not usually endogamous, and, so far from having any distaste for alien marriages, makes a regular business of capturing wives. This practice has given rise to one of the forms of infanticide and may well have been the cause of the extinction of the whole tribes in the early struggle for existence. In short, when tribes are left to themselves, they exhibit no inborn tendency to crystallize into castes. In Europe, indeed, the movement has been all in the opposite direction. The tribes consolidated into nations; they do not sink into the political importance of caste."

SIR HENRY SUMNER MAINE'S THEORY.

Sir Henry Sumner Maine suggests that the origin of caste is to be sought in literary fosterage. After pointing out how, under the Brehon Law, the literary foster-father, though he teaches gratuitously, has a claim through life upon portions of the property of the literary foster-son and under the Hindu Law, though the Brahman teacher of Brahman pupils receives no payment for his services, the Hindu Law repeatedly reserves to him a remote succession to their property and how in later days in Ireland the art and knowledge of Brehon Law became hereditary in certain families who were attached to or dependent on the chiefs of particular tribes, and in India, a vast number of trades and professions exercising particular crafts or possessing particular kinds of knowledge became castes, he says:—"We do not, however, thus arrive at a complete account of the growth of those castes which are definite sections of great populations. One only of these castes really survives in India, that of the Brahmans, and it is strongly suspected that the whole literary theory of caste which is of Brahman origin, is based on the existence of the Brahman caste alone. Now the tendency of knowledge to become hereditary is, by itself, consistent with a great variety of religious and literary cultivation; but as a fact, the Brahmans of India are a remarkably homogeneous class, admitting (though no doubt with considerable local qualifications) a general brotherhood of all members of the order." He then thus enlarges his theory:—" While, then, I cannot say that our scanty information respecting changes in the status of the Brehon lawyers helps us much towards a comprehension of the beginnings of caste in the true sense, I certainly think that we learn something more than we knew before from the references in the Brehon tracts to Literary Fosterage. They appear to me to give a new emphasis and point to the rules of Hindu Law respecting the remote succession of the 'spiritual preception' to the property of families. It seems as if in the most ancient state of both systems Literary and Religious fatherhood had been closely assimilated to actual fatherhood. Under these circumstances, if great schools of Vedic learning existed in India in very ancient times, as we have strong reason to think they did, the relation between teacher and pupil would closely follow and imitate the relation between father and son. A great position would thus be formed, with stores of common knowledge, but the tie between the members would not be purely intellectual; it would from the first be conceived as of the nature of kinship. Such a system, as the old idèas decayed, would tend infallibly to become one of real consanguinity. The aptitude for sacred knowledge would come to be thought to run in the blood of sons whose fathers had been instructed in it and none but such sons would be received with the schools. A caste would thus be formed, in the eyes of its members, the type of all castes."

In so far as this theory is based on the idea that community of occupation is the basis of caste, it may be remarked that it has not so far received any support. If this were so, as M. Senart points out, the institution "await mantre moius de tendance a se morceler, a se disloquer ; l'agent qui l'aurait uniffe d'abord en aurait maintenu la cohesion ". Putting it in another way, Sir Herbert Risley says that if the current idea were correct, all cultivators, traders and weavers ought to belong to the same caste, at any rate within the same area ; but every one knows that this is not the case ; that the same occupation embraces a whole crowd of castes, each of which is a close co-operation though the members of each carry on in exactly the same way the avocation that is common to them all. He also points out that the analogy between Indian caste and the trade guilds of Mediæval Europe is misleading. Castes are endogamous, while the trade guilds were not ; then again castes do not admit outsiders into their ranks, while the trade guilds did. This admission of strangers helped the trade guilds to expand and develop. "A caste is an organism of a lower type; it grows by fission and each step in its growth detracts from its power to advance or to even preserve the art which it professes to practise."

Sir Denzil Ibbetson's Theory.

In the Punjab Census Report for 1881, Sir Denzil Ibbetson outlined a somewhat more comprehensive view of caste. The chapter relating to it has been recently reprinted in book form and is easily available for reference. The following passage taken from it sums up his theory:—"Thus, if my theory be correct, we have the following steps in the process by which caste has been evolved in the Punjab:—(1) The tribal divisions common to all primitive societies; (2) the guilds based upon hereditary occupation common to the middle life of all the communities; (3) the exaltation of the priestly office to a degree unexampled in other countries; (4) the exaltation of the Levitical blood by a special insistence upon the necessarily hereditary nature of occupation; (5) the preservation and support of this principle by the elaboration from the theories of the Hindu creed or cosmogony of a purely artificial set of rules, regulating marriage and inter-marriage, declaring certain occupations and foods to be impure and polluting and prescribing the conditions and degree of social intercourse permitted between the several castes. Add to these the pride of social rank and the pride of blood which are natural to man and which alone could reconcile a nation to restrictions at once irksome from a domestic and burdensome from a material point of view; and it is hardly to be wondered at that caste should have assumed the rigidity which distinguishes it in India."

Critics of his Theory.

M. Senart in his criticism of this theory first demurs to the share which he supposes it to assign to Brahmanical influence and challenges the supposition that a strict code of rules, exercising so absolute a dominion over the consciences of men, could be merely a modern invention, artificial in its character and self-regarding in its aims. Then he takes exception to the disproportionate importance which he conceives Sir Denzil Ibbetson to attach a community of occupation, and points out that if this were really the originally binding principle of caste, the tendency towards incessant fission and dislocation would be much less marked: the force that in the beginning united the various scattered atoms would continue to hit them together to the end. Both these criticisms, in Sir Herbert Risley's view, "appear to miss an essential feature in the scheme, the influence of the idea of kinship, which is certainly the oldest and probably the most enduring factor in the caste system, and which seems to have supplied the framework and motive principle of the more modern restrictions based upon ceremonial usage and community of occupation."

CHAPTER IV.

Origin of Caste: Theories of Nesfield and Senart.

Mr. Nesfield's Theory—Critics of his Theory—M. Senart's Theory—Sir Herbert Risley's Criticism.

Mr. Nesfield, to whose theory we have already referred to, assumes the essential unity of the Indian race and appeals to "physiological resemblance" to prove that "for the last three thousand years at least no real difference of blood between Aryan and aboriginal has existed except perhaps in a few isolated tracts". In his opinion the Aryan was thoroughly absorbed by the indigenous population. His theory is best stated in his own words :—

"If it were possible to compress into a single paragraph a theory so complex as that which would explain the origin and nature of the Indian caste, I should attempt to sum it up in some such words as the following :—A caste is a marriage union, the constituents of which were drawn from various different tribes (or from various other castes similarly formed), in virtue of some industry, craft or function, either secular or religious, which they possessed in common. The internal discipline by which the conditions of membership in regard to connubial and convivial rights are defined and enforced, has been borrowed from the tribal period which preceded the period of castes by many centuries, and which was brought to a close by the amalgamation of tribes into a nation under a common sceptre. The differentia of *Caste* as a marriage union consists in some community of function; while the differentia of *Tribe* as a marriage union consisted in a common ancestry, or a common worship or a common totem, or in fact in any kind of common property except that of a common function. Long before castes are formed on Indian soil, most of the Industrial classes to which they now correspond, had existed for centuries, and as a rule most of the industries which they practised were hereditary on the male side of the parentage. These hereditary classes were and are simply the concrete embodiment of those successive stages of culture which have marked the industrial development of mankind in every part of the world. Everywhere (except at least in those countries where he is still a savage), man has advanced from the stage of hunting and fishing to that of Nomadism and cattle grazing and from Nomadism to agriculture proper. Everywhere has the age of metallurgy and of the arts and industries which are coeval with it been preceded by ruder age, when only those arts were known or practised which sufficed for the hunting, fishing and nomad states. Everywhere has the class of ritualistic priests and lettered theosophists been proceded by a class of less cultivated worshippers, who paid simple offerings of flesh and wine to the personified powers of the visible universe without the aid of an hereditary professional priesthood. Everywhere has the class of the nobles and territorial chieftains been preceded by a humbler class of small peasant proprietors who placed themselves under their protection and paid tribute or rank in return. Everywhere has this class of nobles and chieftains sought to ally itself with that of the priests or sacerdotal order; and everywhere has the priestly order sought to bring under its control those chiefs and rulers under whose protection it lives. All these classes then had been in existence for centuries before any such thing as caste was known on Indian soil; and the only thing that was needed to convert them into castes such as they are now, was that the Brahman who possessed the highest of all functions—the priestly—should set the example. This he did by establishing for the first time the rule that no child, either male or female, could inherit the name and status of Brahman unless he or she was of

Brahman parentage on *both* sides. By the establishment of this rule the principle of marriage unionship was superadded to that of functional unionship; and it was only by the combination of these two principles that a caste in the strict sense of the term could or can be formed. The Brahman, therefore, as the Hindu books inform us, was "the first born of castes". When the example had thus been set by an ignorant and overbearing priesthood whose pretensions it was impossible to put down, the other hereditary classes followed in regular order downwards, partly in imitation and partly in self-defence. To the nation mesmerized Brahmans and blinded with superstition and ignorance no other course was open. Immediately behind the Brahman came the Kshatriya, the military chieftain or landlord. He therefore was the "second born of castes". Then followed the Bankers or Upper trading classes (the Agarwal, Khattri, etc.); the scientific musician and singer (Kathak); the writing or literary class (Kayasth); the Bard or genealogist (Bhat); and the class of inferior nobles (Taga and Bhuinhar) who paid no rent to the landed aristocracy. These, then, were the "third born of castes". In all communities, such classes must stand rather high in the scale of social respectability, since the stages of industry or function which they represent are high in proportion; but in India their rank was more precisely defined than elsewhere by the fact that they made a nearer approach than the caste below them to the Brahmanical ideal of personal dignity and purity. Next in order came those artisan classes who were coeval with the age and art of metallurgy; the metallurgic classes themselves; the middle trading classes; the middle agricultural classes who placed themselves under the protection of the Kshatriya and paid him rent in return (Kurmi, Kachhi, Mali, Tamboli); and the middle serving classes such as Napit and Baidya who attended to the bodily wants of their equals and superiors. These then were the "fourth born of castes" and their rank in the social scale has been determined by the fact that their manners and notions are further removed than those of the preceding castes from the Brahmanical ideal. Next came the inferior artisan classes, those which preceded the age and art of metallurgy (Teli, Kumhar, Kalwar, etc.); the partly nomad and partly agricultural classes (Jat, Gujar, Ahir, etc.); the inferior servant classes such as Kahar; and the inferior trading classes such as Bhunja. These then were the "fifth born of castes" and their mode of life is still further removed from the Brahmanical ideal than that of the preceding. The last born, therefore, and therefore the lowest of all the classes, are those semi-savage communities, partly tribes and partly castes, whose function consists in hunting or fishing or in acting as butcher for the general community or in rearing swine and fowls or in discharging the meanest domestic services such as sweeping and washing or in practising the lowest of human arts such as basket-making, hide-tanning, etc. Thus throughout the whole series of Indian castes a double test of social precedence has been in active force, the Industrial and the Brahmanical; and these two have kept pace together almost as evenly as a pair of horses harnessed to a single carriage. In proportion as the function practised by any given caste stands high or low in the scale of industrial development, in the same proportion does the caste itself, impelled by the general tone of society by which it is surrounded, approximate more merely or more remotely to the Brahmanical ideal of life. It is these two criteria combined which have determined the relative ranks of various castes in the Hindu social scale. Outside the caste system altogether stand the few and shattered remains of those aboriginal tribes, out of which the whole series of caste was fashioned by slow degrees, through the example and under the guidance of Brahmanical priesthood. Had the Brahman never come into existence and had his arrogance proved to be less omnipotent than it did, the various industrial classes would never have become stereotyped into castes, and the nation would then have been spared a degree of social disunion to which no parallel can be found in human history. There seems to be no likelihood of castes being banished from Indian soil until Brahmanism itself—the *Fons et origo mali*—has died a natural death by the rise of the scientific spirit, and the fallacy of its pretensions has become an object of general scorn. As soon as the Brahman begins to disappear the rest will follow."

Criticism of His Theory.

It will be seen that Mr. Nesfield's theory assumes rather than explains. It is more a classification of castes than an attempt at tracing the origin or evolution of caste generally. It takes for granted what it has to solve. The idea of the essential unity of the Indian race which underlies his theory has yet to be proved. As a matter of fact, what has been studied in connection with the physical anthropology of the Indian castes and tribes goes against his basic assumption. It is precisely on this study that Sir Herbert Risley rests his own theory as we will see presently. As Sir Herbert rightly insists, "a theory which included in the same categories the Dom and the Teli, the Banjara and the Khetri and the Kayasth must, in the race for acceptance, lose a good deal of ground at the start." Mr. Nesfield's classification, moreover, is based solely on occupation, and it expresses his conviction that "function and function only, as I think, was the foundation upon which the whole caste system of India was built up". As we have seen above, occupation alone does not and cannot answer for the origin of caste. Mr. Nesfield does not suggest why the groups he mentions, and which he says occur all over the world, became hardened into castes in India. Why is it that in India alone their members are absolutely forbidden to intermarry? Mr. Nesfield replies without hesitation that the whole series of matrimonial taboos which constitute the caste system are due to the initiative of the Brahmans. According to him, they introduced for their own purposes, and in order to secure the dignity and privileges of their own caste, the rule that a Brahman could only marry a Brahman, and all other classes, who upto that time had intermarried freely followed their example, "partly in imitation and partly in self-defence". The proposition recalls, as Sir Herbert Risley well puts it, the short way that writers of the eighteenth century were apt to take with historical problems, and reminds one of Bolingbroke's easy assertion that the sacred literature of Egypt was invented by the priests. It is grossly unscientific to assume large ethnological facts or great historical events and Mr. Nesfield's theory does both with an ease which is truly remarkable.

M. Senart's Theory.

Far different is the theory of M. Senart, which is perhaps the most widely known on the subject. It is elaborated at great length by him in his scholarly work *Les Castes Dans L'inde.* Extracts from it and a general summary of the theory itself are given by Sir Herbert Risley in his *People of India*. Briefly put, M. Senart's view is that caste is the normal development of ancient Aryan institutions, which assumed this form in the struggle to adapt themselves to the conditions with which they came into contact in India. He develops this proposition relying greatly upon the parallelism that may be traced between the social organization of the Hindus and that of the Greeks and Romans in the earlier stages of national development. He points out the close correspondence that exists between the three series of groups—*Gens*, *Curia*, *Phatria*, *Phyle* in Greece; and family, Gotra, Caste in India. Going further into the subject, he seeks to show from the records of classical antiquity that the leading principles which underlie the caste system form part of a stock of usage and tradition common to all branches of the Aryan people. Thus, according to him, endogamy, the chief characteristic of caste, was not unknown to the Greeks and the Romans. The Athenian *Yeros* [illegible] the Roman *Gens* were not unlike the Indian *Gotra*. He points out that no Roman matron who figures in classical literature bears the same gentile name as her husband. At Athens the membership of the *phatria* was, in Demosthenes' time, restricted to offspring of the families belonging to the group. In Rome the fight between the Plebians and Patricians in regard to the *Jus Connubi* shows, according to him, how the patricians were endeavouring to guard the endogamous rights of their order. The Roman *Conferratio* has its parallel in the connubial meal so well known in India. As with marriage, so with food. The prohibition on eating with members of another caste or partaking food prepared by a man of lower caste recalls the religious significance which the Aryans attached to the common meal of the household. Cooked at the sacred fire, it symbolized the unity of the family, its life in the present, its ties with the past. In Rome as in India daily libations were offered to ancestors and the funeral feasts of the Greeks and Romans correspond to the *Sraddah* of Hindu usage which, in M. Senart's view, represents an ideal pro longation of the family meal. To the question why the common stock of usage developed in one place castes and in another nations, M. Senart suggests the answer "L'Inde ne sest elence ni a l'idec de l'etat in a l'idec de la patric. Au lieu de se tendre, le cadre s'y ressere. Au sain des republiques antiques la rotion des classes tend a se resudre dans l'idec plus large de la cite : dans l Inde ell s'accuse, elle tenda se circonscrire dans les cloisens etroites de la caste. N'oublions pas quici les immigrants se re'pandaient sur une aire immense ; les groupments trop vasted etaient condamnes a se disperser. Dans cete circonstance les inclinations particularishes puiserent un supplement de force." Distribution over a wide area, tending to multiply groups : contact with the aborigines, encouraging pride of blood : the idea of ceremonial purity, leading to the employment of the indigenous races in occupations involving manual labour. while the higher pursuits were reserved for the Aryans : the influence of the doctrine of metempsychosis,* which assigns to every man a definite status determined by the inexorable law of *Karma* : the absence of any political power to draw the scattered groups together ; and the authority which the Brahmanical system gradually acquired—these seem to be the main factors of M. Senart's theory.

Sir Herbert Risley's Criticism.

Sir Herbert Risley urges in favour of M. Senart's view that evolution, especially social evolution, is a gradual and complex process, that many causes work together to produce the final result, and that the attempt to reduce them to a single formula carries with it its own reputation. On the other hand, he points out —agreeing with Dr. Fick—that if caste were a normal extension of the ancient Aryan family system, the absence of any traces of this tendency in the Vedas is hardly accounted for by the statement that development proceeded so slowly, and was based on such primitive and instructive impulses, that we could hardly expect to find any tangible indication of it in a literature like that of the hymns. Very similar criticism has been offered by Dr. A. A. Macdonell and Dr. A. B. Keith. "To assume, with Senart," they say, "that the family was the basis of caste is difficult in face of the late appearance of words for family and of stress on family." Bougle also criticizes M. Senart's theory that the origin of the caste system is to be traced to the ancient Aryan family, pointing out that in many ways the part played by the Aryan conquerors has been exaggerated. Sir Edward Gait, who has recently written on the subject, adds that it may now be regarded as proved that the caste system is by no means an exclusively Aryan product. In the matter of religion also the influence of aborigines is well marked. Many of the Hindu deities are of aboriginal origin; and even the idea of metempsychosis is foreign to Vedic Hinduism. The intense desire for a son as a means of spiritual benefit is far from being peculiar to the Aryan Hindu. It is shared by many races all over the world. Among the Buttaks of Sumatra, for example, "it is deemed absolutely necessary to one's well being, both in this world and the next, to have children, no matter how they are begotten." The ideas regarding purity and pollution are less fully developed in the North of India than in the South, where the population is almost wholly Dravidian.

CHAPTER V.

Origin of Caste :
Sir Herbert Risley's Theory.

Sir Herbert Risley's Theory—Race Distinction—His Theory criticized—Mr. Ramprasad Chanda's. Theory.

Sir Herbert Risley who regards the origin of caste "from the nature of the case an insoluble problem" puts forward a "conjecture" as he calls it, derived from the analogy of observed facts. He bases this conjecture, firstly, upon the correspondence that can be traced between certain caste gradations and certain variations of physical type ; secondly, on the development of mixed races from stocks of different colour ; and thirdly, on the influence of fiction. He thus elaborates his theory :—

"In the case of a complex phenomenon, such as caste, to the formation of which a number of subtle tendencies must have contributed, all that we can hope to do is to disentangle one or two leading ideas and to show how their operation may have produced the state of things that actually exists. Following out this line of thought it seems possible to distinguish two elements in the growth of caste sentiment : a basis of fact and a superstructure of fiction. The former is widespread if not universal ; the latter is peculiar to India. Whenever in the history of the world one people has subdued another, whether by active invasion or by gradual occupation of their territory, the conquerors have taken the women of the country as concubines or wives but have given their own daughters in marriage only among themselves. Where the two peoples are of the same age, or, at any rate, of the same colour, this initial stage of what we have called hypergamy soon passes away and complete amalgamation takes place. Where, on the other hand, marked distinctions of race colour intervene, and especially if the dominant people are continuously recruited by men of their own blood, the course of evolution runs on different lines. The tendency then is towards the formation of a class of half-breeds, the result of irregular unions between men of higher and women of the lower, who marry only among themselves and are, to all intents and purposes, a caste. In this literal or physiological sense caste is not confined to India. It occurs in a pronounced form in the Southern States of the American Commonwealth where Negroes intermarry with Negroes and the various mixed races, mulattoes, quadroons and octoroons, each have a sharply restricted *jus connubii* of their own and are absolutely cut off from legal unions with white races. Similar phenomena may be observed among the half-breeds of Canada, Mexico and South America and among the Eurasians of India who do not intermarry with natives and only occasionally with pure-bred Europeans. In each of these cases the facts are well known. The men of the dominant race took to themselves women of the subject race and the offspring of these marriages intermarried for the most part only among themselves. The Eurasians of Ceylon, who are known locally as "Burghers" are a notable example of the formation of a caste in the manner here described. During the Dutch occupation of Ceylon (1656—1795) very few Dutchmen settled in the Island. This fact, combined with tremendous penalties imposed by the puritanical Dutch laws on the sin of fornication, induced many of the Colonists to marry Singalese women of the higher castes. The descendants of these marriages ranked as Dutch citizens and very soon crystallized into a caste disdaining further alliances with the natives and marrying only among themselves. Conscious of their legitimate parentage and proud of title which recalls their Dutch ancestry, the "Burghers" of Ceylon now form a distinct and independent class standing apart from both Europeans and natives and holding a position far superior to that of the Eurasians in India. Illustrations of the same process may be observed in the Himalayas where, if anywhere in India, the practices recorded with exaggerated precision in the Indian law books still survive. The Dogras of the Kangra Hills and Khas of Nepal are believed to be the offspring alliances between conquering Rajputs and women of more or less Mongoloid descent. In the case of Nepal *Hodgson* has described at length the conditions of these unions which correspond in principle with those of the traditional system of Manu. Working from this analogy, it is not difficult to construct the outlines of the process which must have taken place when the second wave of Indo-Aryans first made their way into India through Giljit and Chitral. At starting they formed a homogeneous community, scantly supplied with women, which speedily outgrew its general habitat. A company of the more adventurous spirits set out to conquer for themselves new domains among the conquering Dravidians. They went forth as fighting men taking with them few women or none at all. They subdued the inferior race, established themselves as conquerors and captured women according to their needs. Then they found themselves cut off from their original stock partly by the distance and partly by the alliances they had contracted. By marrying the captured women they had, to some extent, modified their original type ; but a certain pride of blood remained to them, and when they had bred females enough to serve their purposes and to establish a distinct *jus connubii*, they closed their ranks to all further intermixture of blood. When they did this, they became a caste like the castes of the present day. As their numbers grew, their cadets again sallied forth in the same way and became the founders of the Rajput and pseudo-Rajput houses all over India. In each case complete amalgamation with the inferior race was averted by the fact that the invaders only took women and did not give them. They behaved, in fact, towards the Dravidians whom they conquered in exactly the same way as some planters in America behaved to the African slaves whom they imported. This is a rough statement of what may be taken to be the ultimate basis of caste, a basis of caste common to India and to certain stages of society all over the world. The principle upon which the system rests is the sense of distinctions of race indicated by differences of colour—a sense which, while too weak to preclude the men of the dominant race from intercourse with the women whom they have captured, is still strong enough to make it out of the question that they should admit the men whom they have conquered to equal rights in the matter of marriage.

Race Distinction.

Once started in India, the principle was strengthened, perpetuated and extended to all ranks of society by the fiction that people, who speak a different language, dwell in a different district, worship different gods, eat different food, observe different social customs, follow a different profession, or practise the same profession in a slightly different way, must be so unmistakably aliens by a blood that intermarriage with them is a thing not to be thought of. Illustrations of the working of this fiction have been given above in the description of the various types of caste and might be multiplied indefinitely. Its precise origin is necessarily uncertain. All that can be said is that fictions of various kinds have contributed largely to the development of early societies in all parts of the world, and that their appearance is probably due to that tendency to vary, and to perpetuate beneficial variations which seems to be a law of social, no less than of physical, development. However this may be, it is clear that the growth of caste instinct must have been greatly promoted and stimulated by certain characteristic peculiarities of the Indian intellect—its lax hold of facts, its indifference to action, its absorption in dreams, its exaggerated reverence for tradition, its passion for endless division and sub-division, its active sense of minute technical distinctions, its pedantic tendency to press a principle to its furthest logical conclusion, and its remarkable capacity for imitating and adopting social ideas and usages of whatever origin. It is through this initiative faculty that the myth of the four castes evolved in the first instance by some speculative Brahman and reproduced in the popular versions of the epics which the educated Hindu villager studies as diligently as the English rustic used to read his Bible—has attained its wide currency as the model to which Hindu society ought to conform. That it bears no relation to the actual facts of life is, in the view of its adherence, an irrelevant detail. It descends from remote antiquity; it has the sanction of the Brahman; it is an article of faith; and everyone seeks to bring his own caste within one or other of the traditional classes. Finally, as M. Senart has pointed out, the whole caste system, with its scale of social merits and demerits and its endless gradations of status, is in remarkable accord with the philosophic doctrine of transmigration and Karma. Every Hindu believes that his spiritual status at any given time is determined by the sum total of his past lives: he is born to an immutable Karma, what is more natural than that he should be born into an equally immutable caste?"

His Theory Criticized.

This theory has not obtained universal recognition. It has been criticized in diverse ways. It has been suggested, for instance, that Sir Herbert Risley's theory being based on physical measurements made in Bengal, which are at variance with measurements made in other parts of India, and even in Bengal itself, cannot be accepted as final. Sir Edward Gait, as already stated, thinks that there is not that correlation between caste and status which Sir Herbert alleges to exist. Caste is not nearly so "immutable" as Sir Herbert describes it to be. Finally it is a question if Sir Herbert has not exaggerated the influence of fiction in the domain of caste. But it must be acknowledged that he, of all theorists, endeavoured to rivet attention on the ethnic basis of caste. It is true that some earlier writers had hinted at this factor, but they were no more than unverified conjectures. What Sir Herbert did was to give a tangible basis to their conjectures and to make speculation on the subject take a more fruitful turn.

MR. RAMPRASAD CHANDA'S THEORY.

Mr. Ramprasad Chanda, the Indian scholar, to whose views we have referred to above, propounds a theory of caste which is in some ways a novel one. He suggests that originally there were five and not four castes. These are, according to him, covered by the description Pancha Janah mentioned in the *Rig-Veda*, and explained by Yaska as *Panchamanushya-jatani*, *i.e.*, the five classes of men and explained by him as the four *varnas* with the Nishadas as the fifth. The five classes are the Brahmana, Kshatriya, Vaisya, Sudra and Nishada. Mr. Chanda formulates two migrations of Aryans, one through the north-western passes of India from the far North and the other by the Arabian Sea from Mesopotamia, etc. From the first were evolved, according to him, the Brahmans (through the Rishi clans of Vasishta and others) who are spoken of as white in colour in the *Rig-Veda* (vii. 33. 1) and from the later immigrants, who arrived by the sea, were derived the Kshatriyas, through the warrior clan of the Kanwa and Vishvamitra, some of whom were later absorbed into the Brahmian hierarchy. These were black in colour. Another section of these self-same immigrants was, according to him, the Vaisyas who became the "tax-paying subject section". The Sudras, according to him, were also Aryans, whether of the first or second group it is not mentioned by him, and represent those who had been enslaved as the result of the internecine wars of the Aryans. The fifth class, the Nishadas, are identified by him with the pre-Dravidians of Thurston and other writers who are described as "Dasyas", "Unaryas", "Anasikas", etc., in the *Rig-Veda*. All these five classes, according to him, "differed from one another in colour (*varna*) and other prominent physical features." This, "the sense of distinctions of race indicated by differences of colour, to use the language of Risley, is the "basis of fact" in the development of caste system ....The conception of the identity of racial or colour difference and social difference was extended to them by fiction and the Vaisyas and Sudras were recognized as separate *varnas* or colours. With these two elements, fact and fiction, was combined a third element, heredity of function, copied from the Rishi clans. Colour or race differences, real and fancied, together with hereditary function gave birth to the caste system. But as newer groups formed or attached themselves to the Arya nations, the absurdity of regarding them all as different colours or *varnas* was recognized, and the theory of *Varna Sankara* or mixed caste was started to explain their origins."

Though Mr. Chanda quotes a number of Sanskrit texts in support of his theory, there are many points still remaining to be cleared in regard to it. Thus, it is made clear by him how the Vaisyas branched off from the Rajanyas and how they came to be regarded as a separate *varna*. They were *ex hypothesi* of the same colour, *i.e.*, physical bearing as the Rajanyas. Then again, if they branched off from the Rajanyas, why is it that the *Kathaka Samhita* (xi. 6) terms them 'white' (Sukla), while it describes the Rajanya as 'swarthy' (Dhumra). The theory, on the whole, requires much clearer elaboration and stronger evidence than Mr. Chanda has been able to adduce in support of it, if it is to maintain its ground.

CHAPTER VI.

Origin of Caste: The Indian Theory.

The Indian Theory—In the Brahmanas—In the Upanishads—In Baudhayana—In the Bhagavad-Gita—Caste in Buddhism—Caste in Jainism, Saivism & Vedanta Sutras—In Kautilya's Arthasastra—In the Laws of Manu—Risley's Criticism—Objections to Risley's View—Summary of Conclusions.

We may now turn from the theories of modern ethnologists and others to the ancient theory elaborated by Indians themselves in their sacred literature. The earliest account of the origin of the Varnas is found in the famous Purusha Hymn of the *Rig-Veda* (x. 90. 11-12). The Hymn thus describes the creation of castes:—

"When they divided the Purusha, into how many parts did they divide him? What was his mouth? What were his arms? What were his thighs and feet called? The Brahman was his mouth, of his arms the Rajanya was made; the Vaisyas were his thighs; the Sudra sprang from his feet." The Hymn has, however, been held by some Oriental Scholars as a later interpolation. But independently of this there is evidence to believe that in the *Rig-Veda* period the idea of a separate Brahman caste differing from the Warrior and Agricultural castes had already been evolved. Professors Macdonnell and Keith who advance this view hold that "the caste system is one that has progressively developed and that it is not legitimate to look in the *Rig-Veda* for the full caste system even of the *Yajur-Veda* ; but at the same time it is difficult to doubt that the system was already well on its way to general acceptance". In the *Yajur-Veda*(Taittiriya Samhita,vii. 1. 1. 4-6)the theory admittedly receives a clearer expression. Here we read " Prajapati desirous of offspring (performed the Agnishtoma Sacrifice) and created Trivrit hymn, God Agni, Gayatri Metre, Rathatara Saman, Brahman among men and goats among brutes from his mouth. As they were created from the mouth therefore they are superior to all others. (He) created Panchadasa hymn, God Indra, Trishtap Metre, Vrihat Saman, Rajanya among men and sheep among brutes from his chest and arms. Therefore they are strong because they have been created from strength (Strong Arms). (He) created Saptadasa hymn, Visvadevas among the gods, Jagati Metre, Vacrupa Saman, Vaisya among men and cows among brutes from the belly. As they have been created from the storehouse of food (belly) so they are the food (or intended to be enjoyed by others). Therefore, they (Vaisyas) are more numerous than others (among men) because many gods were created. (He) created Ekavamsa hymn, Anushtap Metre, Vairaja Saman, Sudra among men and horse among brutes from his feet. Therefore the Sudra and the horse are dependent on other (castes). As no god was created from the feet, so the Sudra is not competent to perform sacrifice. As the

Sudra and the horse were created from the feet, so they live by exerting their feet."

IN THE BRAHMANAS.

The *Brahmanas* contain repeated references to this creation of the castes. In them castes seem to take a definite shape. In one place (*Satapata Brahmana*, ii. 1-4-12) we read: "with Bhuh! Prajapati generated the Brahman (priesthood); with Bhuvah! the Kshatra (nobility); with Svah! the Vis (the common people). As much as are the Brahmans, the Kshatra and the Vis so much is the Universe; with the universe it (the fire) is accordingly established." At another (viii. 4. 3. 1-20), we have described for us the whole of creation. First the Brahman, then the living beings, then the seven Rishis, then the fathers, then the seasons, then the months, then the Kshatra, then the tame animals, then the Sudra and Arya, then one-hoofed animals, then small animals and then the wild animals.

IN THE UPANISHADS.

The *Brihadaranyaka Upanishad* (I. 4. 10-14) describes the creation of the four Varnas and the law in a rather striking manner. In the beginning we are told the Brahman was created, but being one and not strong enough, the most excellent Kshatra was created. Therefore there is nothing beyond the Kshatra and therefore at the Rajasuya the Brahman sits below the Kshatriya. But the Brahman is the birthplace of Kshatra. Therefore though a king exalted, he sits down at the end (of the sacrifice) below the Brahmana as his birthplace. He who wrongs him injures his own birthplace. He becomes worse, because he has injured one better than himself. The Kshatriya was not strong enough. Therefore he created the Vis (people). He was not strong enough. He created the Sudra colour (Varna) as Pushan (Nourisher). This earth verily is Pushan (the nourisher); for the earth nourishes all whatsoever. He was not strong enough. He created further the most excellent Law (Dharma). Law is the Kshatra (power) of the Kshatra, therefore there is nothing higher than tne Law.

The difference of time that separates the theory of creation as outlined in the Vedas from the one that is put forth in the *Brihadaranyaka Upanishad* is perhaps responsible for the outpouring contained in the latter. In the *Rig-Veda*, the Brahman as such is being evolved; in the *Yajur-Veda*, we see the four varnas described as actually separate creations, as distinct from one another as the goat, the sheep, the cow and the horse; this view is not altogether given up in the *Brahmanas*, but in the Upanishadic age it is felt necesary, in keeping with the speculations of the period, to insist on the essential equality, if not the oneness, of all castes, each being created as required for the good of society, the Law being above all. The special glorification of the Law which the *Brihadaranyaka Upanishad* indulges in shows that at the time it was composed, it was felt that in the eye of the Law all were equal and none could pretend to a higher status over another. The Kshatriya takes, we are specially told, the first place at one time in the Rajasuya Sacrifice, but comes after the Brahman at its end. He is not to speak ill of the Brahman because he is his birthplace; nay, we are abjured, he injures one better than himself. Whether we may deduce from this that though a separate creation is predicated for the Kshatriya, he was really descended from the Brahman, and likewise the Vaisya and the Sudra, in their turn, is open to doubt, for the hymn is not explicit in regard to the two latter.

IN BAUDHAYANA.

We seem to get to a further stage in the writings of Baudhayana (I. 18. 1. 6), Gautama (iv. 24) and Vasishta (II and IV), which can all be referred to the sixth century B.C. They give nearly the same account of the creation of castes and of their different duties. The last of these after stating that "the four castes are distinguished by their origin and by particular sacraments" quotes the texts of the *Rig* and *Yajur-Veda* hymns in support of the statement that "a Sudra shall not receive the sacraments". The reason given is that the Sudra, according to the *Yajur-Veda*, was created "without any metre". It is, perhaps, inferable from this that the Sudras had by Vasishta's time become a distinct caste or representative heads of a caste going under that name. It is significant that the Yajus text says that "they are not competent to perform sacrifice" while Vasishta extends their disability by saying that "they shall not receive the sacraments". All the same he insists that "truthfulness, suppression of anger, liberality, abstention from injuring living beings and the procreation of offspring are duties common to all castes."

In the Bhagavad-Gita.

When we come to the period of *Bhagavad-Gita*, we find that though the idea of creation still persists, the exaltation of the Dharma is carried still further. The position taken in the *Brihadaranyaka Upanishad* is emphasized, if not enlarged. The castes have not only their particular qualities but also their particular duties. And then we are told (*Bhagavad-Gita*, III. 35 *et seq.*) that the performance of one's own duty though imperfect is better than the performance of another's duty though well performed. Death in performing one's own duty is preferable, the performance of the duties of others is dangerous. The theory of creation is referred to in two places (Ch. IV. 13 & Chap. XVIII. 41) and these indicate the position of the *Bhagavad-Gita* in regard to Caste. In the first Sri Krishna says: " The four-fold division of castes was created by me according to the apportionment of qualities and duties." In the second he adds:—" The duties of Brahmanas, Kshatriyas and Vaisyas and of Sudras, too, terror of your foes! are distinguished according to the qualities born of nature. Tranquillity, restraint of senses, penance, purity and forgiveness, straightforwardness, also knowledge, experience and belief (in a future world), this is the natural duty of the Brahmanas. Valour, glory, courage, dexterity, non-shirking from battle, gifts, exercise of bodily power, this is the natural duty of the Kshatriyas. Agriculture, breeding cattle, trade, (this) is the natural duty of the Vaisyas. And the natural duty of the Sudras, too, consists in service. (Every) man intent on his own respective duties obtains perfection. Listen, now, how one intent on one's own duty obtains perfection. Worshipping, by (the performance of) his own duty, him from whom all things proceed, and by whom all this is permeated, a man obtains perfection. One's duty, though defective, is better than another's duty well performed. Performing the duty prescribed by nature one does not incur sin." As Telang points out, in the *Bhagavad-Gita*, the duties of the different castes do not overlap. In Chapter X, in which the best of everything is mentioned, the Brahman is not declared to be the best of the castes. On the other hand, the King is mentioned as the highest among men. On the contrary, in the latter verse, we find the famous saying "The Brahman is the head of the castes". The *Bhagavad-Gita* and Buddha agree first in their protests against the authority of the Vedas, and second in their conception of the true view of the differences of caste. The *Gita* shelves caste, while Buddha rejects it. The *Gita* does not totally root out caste, but it places it on a less untenable basis. In Telang's view the *Gita* is really the predecessor of the Buddhist attempt to do away with caste.

Caste in Buddhism.

Buddha's attitude towards caste is well brought out by his definition of an outcaste, which is illustrated by the story of Chandala who was reborn in the Brahman world. In the *Sutta Nipata*, in which the story is told, we read : "Not by birth does one become an outcaste, not by birth does one become a Brahman ; by deeds one becomes an outcaste, and by deeds one becomes a Brahmana. Buddha himself is neither a Brahman, nor a king's son, nor a Vessa (Vaisya), but a wandering Mendicant". The *Sutta Nipata* again asserts : " Do not ask about descent, but ask about conduct ; from wood it is true fire is born ; (likewise) a firm *muni*, although belonging to a low family, may become noble, when restrained (from sinning) by humility. One who has seen Buddha is appeased, even if he be of black origin." The Buddhist Sutras maintain that the truth proclaimed by Buddha is open to all. According to the Vinaya texts, members of the four castes renounce their names and their lineage when they become Buddhist monks.

Caste in Jainism, Saivism and Vedanta Sutras.

The Jain attitude is equally clear. In the *Jaina Sutras* the story is told of the monk Harikesa Bala, born in the family of Svapakesa —the lowest of lowly castes—converting a Brahmana. The self-same *Sutras* state that a Brahmana, Kshatriya, an Ugra or a Lichchavi, when entering the order is not stuck up on account of his Gotra. Their reasoning is direct and simple. If there were only one soul, these could not be of Brahmanas, Kshatriyas, Vaisyas and Sudras. This indifference to caste was adopted by the Saivas, according to whom, men of different castes may become Brahmanas. According to the *Vedanta Sutras* of Badarayana, which in date are posterior to the *Bhagavad-Gita*, difference of castes results from the soul's connection with a body, though all souls are part of Brahman and equal.

In Kautilya's Arthasastra.

Kautilya's *Arthasastra*, though a work of much later date than the *Bhagavad-Gita*, which, according to Telang, " must be earlier than the third century B.C., though it is impossible to say at present, how much earlier", takes a view of castes which is in some respects in keeping with it. The duties it assigns to the four castes greatly overlap and the functions of the Vaisyas and Sudras are enlarged to an extent unknown before. It says :—" The duty of the Brahman is study, teaching, performance of sacrifice, officiating in other's sacrificial performance and the giving and receiving of gifts. That of a Kshatriya is study, performance of sacrifice, military occupation and protection of life. That of a Vaisya is study, performance of sacrifice, giving gifts, agriculture, cattle breeding and trade. That of a Sudra is the serving of twice-born, agriculture and cattle-breeding and trade, profession of artisans and court-bards." When compared with the duties assigned to the four castes in the *Gita*, this description which was probably quite true of the period to which it belongs,the period of Chandragupta, is certainly a widely enlarged one. Despite this difference, we find the same insistence here, on the performance of one's own duty as we find in the *Gita*. Thus we read in the same Chapter (III) of the *Arthasastra* :—" The observance of one's own duty leads one to Svarga and infinite bliss. When it is violated, the world will come to an end owing to confusion of castes and duties. Hence the king shall never allow the people to swerve from their duties ; for whoever upholds his own duty even adhering to the customs of the Aryas, and following the rules of caste and divisions of religious life, will surely be happy both here and hereafter." The words of Vasishta, prescribing the duties common to all castes, which we have quoted already, also seem to find an echo in the *Arthasastra*, for we are told that " harmlessness, truthfulness, purity, freedom from spite, abstinence from cruelty and forgiveness are duties common to all castes and orders."

In the Laws of Manu.

In the *Laws of Manu*, which in its present form probably dates from 200 A.D, we have the old theory of the creation of the four castes set down in the traditional manner, but there is a still (Books I to XI) further enlargement in the duties assigned to each of them. Thus the Brahman's duties include study, teaching, sacrifice, officiating at another's sacrifices, making and receiving gifts, living by inheritance, occupancy, lawful gleaning, and gathering or receipt of what is given unasked. In default he may become a soldier, or till the ground or breed cattle. The Kshatriya is to govern, and fight and make conquests, to learn the management of chariots and the use of the bow, to stand firm in battle and not to turn back, to protect the people, to abstain from sensual pleasures, and to pay obedience to Brahmans. The Vaisyas are to tend cattle, to lend money, to trade, and to cultivate the land. The Sudra is to serve the three other castes. Comparing these duties with those assigned to the same castes in the *Arthasastra*, we find that within the four centuries which lie between it and the *Laws of Manu*, we find that the Brahman's duties are enlarged in a variety of ways, including agriculture, soldiering, and living a life of ease on patrimony or bounty, the Kshatriya is confined to his royal duties, the Vaisya likewise has no sacrifices to offer and is no more than a mere trader or cultivator and the Sudra is to rest content with serving the three others. This enlargement and contraction of duties is probably based on the actual condition of the age. Undoubtedly the mixed castes bulk large in the pages of Manu. A comparison in this respect with the Sutra writers, Vasishta or Baudhayana, is instructive. Such a comparison would be more instructive if we had the *Manavya Sutra*, on which our present Manu is apparently based, which unfortunately is not now available to us. A careful study of Manu discloses the fact that intermingling between the four castes and their crosses had in fact become so common that rules had to be laid down for determining the status of the children born of the various kinds of unions then in vogue. It seems inferable that by the time of Manu, caste came to be stereotyped in its present form, though the process had been going on for some centuries. *VARNA*, colour, the original distinction based on the physical characteristic of the colour of the skin, we find in the *Rig-Veda* gives place in *Manu* to *JATI* or the act of becoming, *i.e.*, becoming something definite in the social scale as worked out by the process of Brahmanization of the non-Aryan races. This process is, as we have seen, not yet complete and is still going on. But the main lines on which it has been going on had been perceived and understood thoroughly in the time of Manu and the rules worked out by him fixed, for all time to come, the rights and duties of the tribal, mixed and degraded castes that had come to exist in the land.

Risley's Criticism.

Manu's theory of the origin of caste, as will readily be seen, is no new thing. In essence it is the same, which we find given expression to in the early writers we have quoted above. The theory as attributed to him has been described by some as fantastic and grotesque. But as Sir Henry Risley points out there is an element of historic truth in it : it shows us that at the time Manu's treatise was compiled, about the 2nd century A.D., there must have existed an elaborate and highly developed social system, including tribal, national and functional groups. Assuming that this was so, and that society then was, as now, a medley of divers and heterogeneous groups apparently not so strictly and uniformly endogamous as the castes of to-day but containing within themselves the germs out of which the modern system has developed by natural and insensible stages, the question is from what source is the theory of the four castes derived? Sir Herbert Risley thinks it possible that it "may be nothing more than modified version of the division of society into four classes—priests, warriors, cultivators and artisans—which appears in the sacerdotal literature of ancient Persia."

Objections to Risley's View.

This theory, however, has no support anywhere. It is based on altogether insufficient data and is confessedly no more than a mere "conjecture". There is nothing to show that the Iranian Groups with the exception of the Athawans or priests, were endogamous though Sir Herbert Risley thinks that "it is possible that their matrimonial relations may have been governed by the practice of hypergamy which is apt to arise under a regime of castes as distinguished from classes" The next few sentences show how entirely *a priori* is the character of the argument adopted. "The conjecture is," says Sir Herbert, "the relatively modern compilers of the law books, having become acquainted with the Iranian legend, were fascinated by its assertion of priestly supremacy and made use of it as the basis of the theory of which they attempted to explain the manifold complexities of the caste system. The procedure is characteristic of Brahmanical literary methods." The progressive development of the Caste System as disclosed by the texts we have quoted above, shows how untenable this theory is. Professors Macdonald and Keith think that there is no probability in the view that the names of the old classes were later superimposed artificially on a system of castes that were different from them in origin. "We cannot say," they add, "that the castes existed before the classes and that the classes were borrowed by India from Iran as Risley maintains, ignoring the early Brahmana evidence for the Varnas and treating the transfer as late."

SUMMARY OF CONCLUSIONS.

We may now briefly sum up our conclusions. These are that caste is not unknown out of India; that caste in India was not, as has been said, the "invention" of the Brahman, but the result of contact between Aryan and non-Aryan races, the latter contributing as much towards its formation as the former; that marked physical differences between the races in India no less than the peculiar social tendencies they exhibited contributed thus in developing the idea of caste; that in the beginning it was probably purely functional in character; that in later times as the area of contact grew, the growth of national, tribal, degraded and mixed castes went on practically unchecked; that possibly during this period the functional basis changed into a hereditary one, owing as much to the influence of systematizing legists as to the influence of the religious doctrine of Karma; that the development of caste in India has been both gradual and unaffected by foreign influences; that from the beginning there have been protests against its tendency to fission and debasement of human character; that the tendency of the teachings of the Upanishads and the *Bhagavad-Gita* was to place caste on a less untenable basis; that the Jain, Buddhist, Saiva and Vedanta schools of thought altogether ignore caste; that Manu's theory should only be treated assuming the conditions of his time; that in so far as Manu follows the older writers in dividing castes into Brahman, Kshatriya, Vaisya and Sudra he is only following the usual formula enunciated by them and trying to adjust the conditions of his own time with the formula as enunciated by them; that formula having been evolved when function probably formed the basis of caste,—should not be construed literally and that regarded from any point of view the division itself is not borrowed but indigenous.

CHAPTER VII.

Effects of Caste.

Some Divergent Views—James Mill, Colebrook Elphinstone, Sir Henry Maine, Sir Rabindranath Tagore, Comte, Robertson, Abbe Dubois, Sir Alfred Lyall, Dr. J. N. Farquhar—Right Hand and Left Hand Castes—Its Comparative Unimportance To-day.

As may be readily imagined the peculiarities of the caste system have afforded occasion for the propounding of the most divergent views as to its influence on Hindu progress. We have space here only to set down a few of these opposing views to indicate the position assumed by the respective writers. James Mill has denounced it as a great political blunder, fatal to free competition and opposed to individual happiness. This view, however, assumes a state of facts which is undeniably non-existent.

As Colebrook and Elphinstone have pointed out, the restrictions of caste in regard to occupations have had no practical effect on the people of this country. Any one has been free to follow any occupation he chooses and even the Brahman has been since at least the time of Manu (III. 151-166) free to take to any occupation he desires to choose. Sir Henry Maine described caste as "the most disastrous and blighting of human institutions". Others like Sir Rabindranath Tagore have referred to the " immutable and all-pervading system of caste" and pointed out how it has retarded the growth of nationality in India. This view, however, has been subjected to acute criticism by Sir Herbert Risley in one of the best chapters of the book *The People of India* and his conclusions may be stated in a few words. Caste in particular, writes Sir Herbert Risley, seems at first sight to be absolutely incompatible with the idea of nationality, but the History of the Marathas suggests that a caste or a group of castes might develop into a nation and that the caste organization itself might be employed with effect to bring about such a consummation. A recent missionary critic of note has stigmatized caste as a pontifical denial of the brotherhood of man. Another who is alive to the advantages that caste secured to the Hindus generally in its earlier stages, thinks that its religious basis is "clearly dying" and broadly suggests that it has outlived its usefulness. On the other hand, there are not wanting observers who hold views directly opposed to these. Compte's appreciation of caste is well known. He regards the hereditary transmission of functions under the rule of a sacerdotal class as a necessary and universal stage of social progress greatly modified by war and colonization. The morality of caste was, he contends, an improvement on what preceded; but its permanence was impossible because, "the political rule of intelligence is hostile to human progress". The seclusion of women and the preservation of industrial inventions were, according to him, features of caste; and the higher priests were also magistrates, philosophers, artists, engineers and physicians. The Historian Robertson and the French Missionary the Abbe Dubois have regarded caste as the great safeguard of social tranquillity and therefore as the indispensable condition of the progress in certain arts and industries which the Hindus have undoubtedly made. The Abbe Dubois, indeed, devotes a whole chapter of his work to prove his contention that "it is caste authority which by means of its wise rules and prerogatives, preserves good order, suppresses vice and saves Hindus from sinking into a state of barbarism." He thinks that much of the European criticism levelled against caste is the result of the imperfect knowledge of the Hindu people and the spirit and character of their institutions. "I believe," he writes deliberately, "caste division to be in many respects the *chef-d'œuvre*, the happiest effort of Hindu legislation. I am persuaded that it is simply and solely due to the distribution of the people into castes that India did not lapse into a state of barbarism, and that she preserved and perfected the arts and sciences of civilization whilst most other nations of the earth remained in a state of barbarism. I do not consider it to be free from many great drawbacks; but I believe that the resulting advantages, in the case of a nation constituted like the Hindus, more than outweigh the resulting evils." Writing nearly a century later, Sir Alfred Lyall uses language almost nearly the same as the Abbe. "All our European experiments," he writes, "in Social Science have taught us the unwisdom of demolishing old world fabrics which no one is yet prepared to replace by anything else. Caste, for instance, looks unnecessary and burdensome, it is wildly abused by Europeans, to whom the Brahmanic rules of behaviour seem unmeaning and unpractical; but these things will tumble quite fast enough without our knocking at their keystones by premature legislation......We have ourselves to overcome the rather superficial contempt which an European naturally conceives for societies and habits of thoughts different from those within the range of his own ordinary experience and also to avoid instilling too much of the destructive spirit into the mind of Young India, remembering that for English and natives the paramount object is now to preserve social continuity."

Dr. J. N. Farquhar who thinks that the religious basis of caste is dead or dying under the stress of modern conditions, freely concedes that caste during the earlier stages did much good to the people who came into its fold. First, according to him it proved a thoroughly social institution, being a great advance on the simple arrangements of the Aryans when they entered India. It sought to absorb the aborigines instead of destroying them as has been done in many lands. Secondly, it has preserved the Hindu race and its civilization along with its family institutions. But for this powerful protection, Hindu culture would have been overwhelmed by the terrific political storms of the centuries and the race could have survived only in fragments. Thirdly, caste did for many centuries in India the work which was done in Europe by the mediæval trade guilds. Fourthly, caste has also served to some extent the purpose of a poor law in India; for the well-to-do members of the caste fulfil in some degree at least the duty of providing for those members who have fallen into indigence. Another European observer sums up the case for caste in a few sentences which may be quoted in this connection. "The caste organization," says the author of 'A Vision of India', "is to the Hindu his club, his trades union, his benefit society, his philanthropic society. The obligation to provide for kinsfolk and friends in distress is universally acknowledged nor can it be questioned that it is due to that recognition of the strength of family ties, and of the bonds created by the Associations and common pursuits which is fostered by the caste principle. An Indian, without caste, as things stand at present, is not quite easy to imagine."

This subject of the social and economic value of caste however opens up a great line of investigation—how far the caste system has absorbed the guilds of old India—and cannot be pursued just now. The importance of the subject deserves separate and detailed treatment.

I would invite the attention of readers to this and other matters connected with this subject and request them to take them up for study and investigation. The subject, as I have said, is a vast one and requires closer critical attention at the hands of scholars in this country. I would, for instance, suggest a paper on caste as found in the Tamil writers from early times to about 1800 A.D. Similarly there is ample scope for a paper on "Caste" in the Telugu writers beginning from 13th century onwards to the close of the Vijayanagar period. It is to be hoped that students thirsting for research will turn their attention to this subject, as it is one that requires more light to be thrown on it. The subject is of immense practical importance, and I trust my suggestion will be taken up by some at least of our members.

Right Hand and Left Hand Castes.

A point of some interest, if not of importance, in connection with caste is the origin of distinction of castes into right hand and left hand. This distinction is found practically all over Southern India and is referred to in lithic inscriptions found in many districts of Mysore and Madras, dating from about the 11th century A.D. In the Mysore State the agricultural, artisan and trading castes are termed *Panas* or professions, which are 18 in number. These Panas are divided into two divisions called Bala-gai and Yada-gai (corresponding to Tamil—valan-gai and edan-gai) or Right and Left hands. A large number of castes belong to one or other of these divisions. Although the right hand and left hand factions are said to include only 18 trades, there are many castes which adhere to one side or the other but their numbers do not seem to be taken into account. All Brahmins, Kshatriyas and most of the Sudras are considered neutral. It is impossible to obtain authentic lists of the castes belonging to the two divisions. The lists vary from locality to locality. The following is one of those commonly given in the State :—

RIGHT HAND DIVISION.

Banajiga	Traders
Okkaliga	Cultivators
Ganiga (Ontethu)	Oil men who yoke only one bullock to the mill
Rangare	Dyers
Lada	Mahratta Traders
Gujarati	Gujarati Merchants
Kamati	Labourers
Jaina or Komati	Jain Traders or Komati Traders
Kuruba	Shepherds
Kumbara	Potters
Agasa	Washermen
Bestha	Fishermen
Padmasale	A class of Weavers
Nayinda	Barbers
Uppara	Salt-makers
Chitragara	Painters
Golla	Cowherds
Holeya	Agricultural labourers

LEFT HAND DIVISION.

Panchala comprising :—

Badagi	Carpenters
Kanchagara	Copper or Brass Smiths
Kammara	Iron Smiths
Kal-Kutiga	Stone Masons, etc.
Akkasale	Goldsmiths
Bheri	A class of Nagartha traders
Devanga	A class of Weavers
Hegganiga	Oil men who yoke two bullocks to the mill

Golla	Cowherd
Beda	Hunters
Yakula or Toreya	Cultivators or a class of Fishermen
Palli or Tigala	Market Gardeners
Madiga	Chucklers

The Telugu Banajigas and Linga Banajigas are the recognized heads of the right hand division. According to them all the eighteen panas enumerated above belong to them and that 9 panas of the left hand are separate. The Panchalas and Nagarthas who are at the head of the left hand section, contend that the 18 panas are equally divided between the two factions and that the nine enumerated above belong to them. However this may be, the origin or the distinction is buried in obscurity. According to one tradition, it arose from the fact of the Goddess Kali at Conjeevaram placing certain castes on her right hand and certain others on her left. The parties have ever since disputed as to the relative honour accorded to each side. Mr. Rice in the last edition of the *Mysore Gazetteer* suggested that the division was apparently a comparatively modern one, as no mention of it is to be found in any ancient work except for a doubtful passage in the *Mahawanso*. The Abbe Dubois took a similar view. Another writer puts forward that the distinction was the creation of a Chola King. Recently Sir Edward Gait has suggested that the division may be a survival of a dual exogamous grouping which existed before the development of the caste system. There is also a right hand and left hand division of Sakti worshippers, the rites of the former being principally magical, of the latter bloody and licentious. But, as pointed out by Dr. W. H. Wilson, there seems to be no connection between the cases. According to him, further, the division is mainly a struggle for precedence between the artisans and the traders, or between the followers of the old established handicrafts and innovators who brought in exchange of commodities with other parts supported by producers and ministers of luxuries. Whether this is so or not, each party undoubtedly insists on its exclusive rights to certain privileges on all public festivals and ceremonies, and it not unfrequently happens that one side usurps the supposed and jealously guarded rights of the other. On such an occasion a faction fight is sure to occur. "Perhaps the sole cause of the contest is the right to wear slippers or to ride through the streets in a palanquin, or on horseback during marriage festivals. Sometimes it is the privilege of being escorted on certain occasions by armed retainers, sometimes that of having a trumpet sounded in front of a procession, or of being accompanied by native musicians at public ceremonies. Perhaps it is simply the particular kind of musical instrument suitable to such occasions that is in dispute; or perhaps it may be the right of carrying flags of certain colours or of certain devices during these ceremonies." The Abbe Dubois who writes thus adds that he had on several occasions witnessed popular insurrections excited by the mutual pretensions of the two factions. "I have sometimes seen these rioters," he says, "stand up against several discharges of artillery without exhibiting any sign of submission." These faction fights figure prominently in the Madras Records of the 18th century. They have gradually disappeared under the civilizing influence of education and good government; and if they ever occur at all, are confined to the lowest castes forming them and never spread beyond the limits of a village. The distinction between the two factions, however, still exists, though it is of no great practical interest, whether from the social or administrative point of view.

INDEX.

(The figures denote the numbers of pages.)

A

B

B.—(*Contd.*)

C

D

E

F

G

H

I

J

K

L

M

N

O

P

R

R.—(*Contd.*)

S

T

U

V

W

Y

Z